IT'S THE JJAM TEAM

JORDAN JAM

DEDICATION

I dedicate this book to my son Jae and my step daughters Analeigh and Mckinley. I love you all so much and I couldn't ask for more in life then being your mother. You all are such great siblings to Jordan and he is so lucky to have you all.

ACKNOWLEDGEMENT

Thanks to my wonderful blended family that I get to write these adventurous and exciting books.

'What would you like to be called?' dad asked the three little kids

dressed up as superheroes.

'We must have a cool name. We are the superheroes.' Ana said with pride.

Oh, that's right you are cool heroes. What could be your cool name...let me think.'

Dad thought and thought until Jae cried out.

'Dad, we can be JAM.'

'Hahaha...why not jelly too?' Ana giggled.

'JAM as J for Jae, A for Ana and M for McKinley. J.A.M team.
Besides, we all love the Jam.' Jae explained.

'Wow...you are a genius, Jae.' Dad said joyfully.

'Yeah! And we are the mix fruit jam. As half Korean and half-Filipino, with Half Chinese Jam.

'We are the mix Jam, aren't we?' McKinley explained and everybody laughed at the real description.

After that day, the kids called themselves the JAM team. Just like jam, they were sweet to each other and like Jam; they stick close to each other. They were the real-life mix jam.

They loved to play with each other and never quarreled with one another other.

One day, dad called them all to come to him. They came up running to him.

Dad gave everyone some ice cream.

Ice cream was their favorite.

He asked them,

'Well, I was thinking, how about you add another fruit to your JAM team.'

They all paused and tried to think how it is possible. Dad explained and they looked at each other with mixed feelings. 'But dad, we can't add another one to J.A.M. It won't be jam anymore don't you think.' Ana thought.

'I thought you guys are mix fruit jam so wouldn't it be better to have one more?' dad suggested as they all enjoyed the ice cream.

'Hmm...but what would our name become?' Jae asked.

'Well let's see. How about if we have your baby sister we'll call her Jenny and if there will be a baby brother we will call him Jordan. It would be J.J.A.M. The jam team would still be jam.' Dad explained and they looked at each other with mixed feelings.

After a few months, mom and dad entered the house with a small baby in their hands.

All the three kids were curious to see the little one. Once they met Jordan, they were very clear in their feelings. They loved their baby brother Jordan. Jordan became the center of their lives. Jordan was indeed the sweetest. He had all his three siblings head over heels for him. They spoil him with love and kisses. A boss baby of the house of Blended J.J.A.M family.